Open Range

Poetry of the Reimagined West

Open Range

Poetry of the Reimagined West

Edited by Laurie Wagner Buyer & WC Jameson

GHOST ROAD PRESS

Copyright © 2007 by Laurie Wagner Buyer and W.C. Jameson
All rights reserved. Published in the United States of America.
First edition.

No part of this book may be produced or transmitted in any form, or by any means, electronic or mechanical, including photocopying, recording or by any information storage or retrieval system without written permission from the publisher.

Library of Congress Cataloging-in-Publication Data.

Open Range
Ghost Road Press
ISBN   10 digit: 0-9789456-6-2
Library of Congress Control Number: 2007921498

Ghost Road Press
Denver, Colorado

ghostroadpress.com

Contents

Introduction   11

Mike Blakely
Letter to Angelina   13
Slow Falling Rain   14
Uvalde County   16

Laurie Wagner Buyer
Cherry Red Winter   17
On a June Afternoon   18
Cotyledon   19
Witness to a Death   20
Blizzard Night   21
Five-strand with Stays   22
Hay Meadow   23

Jon Chandler
On the Rio Grande at South Fork   24
Texas 1968/1983/1998   25
The Once-Gangly Kid Looks Back   27

Bob Cherry
Collage with Dark Dog   28
Fair Grounds at Fort Worth   29
Innuendo to a Final Frontier   31
Quartet   32
Two Forces   33

Gaydell Collier
Black Hills Evening   34
Scent of Baskets   35
When the Sodergreen House Burned Down   37

John Duncklee
El Corrido de Antonio Beltran — 39
In the Corner — 46

Dan Guenther
About Elk — 47
Hunter — 48
Keeper of the Ute's Winter Moon — 49
When deer move down the mountain — 50

Linda Hussa
The Un-doing of Heaven's Match — 51
Basque Herders — 53
January Gift — 54

W.C. Jameson
The Air — 55
The Headstone — 56
To Beat the Devil — 57
Los Zopilotes — 58
So Much Time Has Passed — 59

Celinda Kaelin
Custer's Boots — 60
Holy Woman Tree — 62
Sundancing at Pine Ridge — 64

Page Lambert
Culling Buffalo at Yellowstone — 68
Dispersal — 69
Even as the Antler — 70

Max McCoy
Summer is short and the night is long   71

Red Shuttleworth
Lyndon Baines Johnson (1928)   76
Elman Card (1937)   77
John Wilkes Booth (1938)   78
Huron "Ted" Waters (1938)   79
Milton Parker Looney (1994)   80

George Sibley
Hartman Rocks   81
Hawks and Haying at Clarke's Ranch   82
On Driving Past the One Hundred Thousandth Roadkill   83
West Elks Haiku   84

Larry D. Thomas
Blue Norther   85
Forgotten Horseshoe   86
Near Pecos   87
Night Goat   88
Sierra Diablo   89

Mark Todd
Mountain Roads   90
Like Sleep, But Brittle   91
Runaway   92

Lori Van Pelt
Snowy Range Moon   94
Tardy Visitor to the Graveyard   95
The Deaf Lady Sings   96

Dale L. Walker
Eldorado   97

Richard S. Wheeler
After I'm Gone   99

Paul Zarzyski
Cowboy Poet Barnstormer   100
Flowering   102
Photo Finish   104
Reminders   106
The Day Beelzebub Gave His Jezebel a Hotfoot   108
Time Travel   112

Contributors Notes   114

Introduction

In his meticulous and thoughtful novel *Second Lives*, award-winning author Richard S. Wheeler depicts one of his characters, Lorenzo Carthage, as a despondent poet who is frustrated by his former idols Emerson and Thoreau, Longfellow and Whittier. As Lorenzo makes his way to the Swallow Café on Cherry Creek in 1880s Denver, he surmises that "what the nation needed was a poetry of the West, unburdened by any rules whatsoever."

Indeed. A search through libraries and bookstores for such a collection of poetry yielded little that was "unburdened by rules," or that connoted the feeling of freedom, of reveling in the thrall of the landscape, the culture, the wildlife. We encountered a variety of poetry, including traditional cowboy evocations of ranch life and trail drives, as well as technically impressive but soulless academic verse. These themes, however, did not reflect an all-encompassing celebration of things Western. What we wanted was the grit and grain of reality, poetry giving voice to the essence of the West, not the mythology. We set out in search of poets who accomplished this, and we found them.

In envisioning this collection, we asked its contributors to follow the precept stated by Wheeler's Lorenzo Carthage: to submit poems that ignore the code and break the rules, poems that challenge the standard notion of the West and Western poetry. We craved poems that jump fences and escape across vast landscapes. Our aesthetic called for poems that embrace the West of personal conviction.

To re-imagine means to think again, to form a mental image of something in a distinctly new way. The twenty poets represented in these pages deliver work that accomplishes this concept in compelling, inspiring, and memorable ways. Here, the reader will find today's authentic, unadulterated West.

—*Laurie Wagner Buyer and W.C. Jameson*

Mike Blakely

Letter to Angelina

Dear Angelina,

I found a payroll for the winter, tending roughstock
out on free range. It's as lonesome as hell in this line camp
out of Elko, but the scenery suits me for a change.

I know you think my life's wasted because I never made any money
that I didn't burn. A cowboy's wage doesn't really suit
a man my age, but I've never taken anything that I didn't earn.

Do you remember how we danced that night in Taos?
I whirled you across the hall. You gave me more
on a dance floor in one evening than I could ever give you at all.

When I woke up this morning the stars were still shining
in a sky of turquoise blue. The snow was so fine,
like white lace on the trees. The first thing I thought about was you.

Angelina, don't remember me unkindly. I didn't mean to let you
down. Whenever I see something beautiful you know it will
always remind me of those times I spent with you in town.

Angelina, I never should have tried to settle down.

Slow Falling Rain

Thunder rumbled in my dreams this morning,
it was distant but plain.
I tried to hold back the day and the dawning,
tried to dream us some rain.

I heard the horses stampede to the stables,
they always know.
Waking up, I saw you in the breeze
at the window with your hair flowing.

>Keep on believing, Amelia,
>I understand your pain.
>You've given up on your own dreams for me,
>you have so little to gain –

>Just let me hold you
>whenever life starts to make you insane.
>Let me love you
>like a slow falling rain.

There's something soothing about the sound of raindrops
playing the old window panes.
There's something real about the ring of the rooftop
singing under the rain.

I believe we can get through the summer.
I believe in this dream.
I believe you're a sight to behold
with the lightning in your eyes gleaming.

>Keep on believing, Amelia,
>I understand your pain.
>You've given up your own dreams for me,
>you have so little to gain—

Just let me hold you
whenever life starts to make you insane.
Let me love you
like a slow falling rain.

Uvalde County

Now the days have been many I've drifted these ranges,
Many's the night I have slept on the ground,
But the sun it won't rise here to darken my shadow,
Uvalde County is where I am bound.

There's a girl I know well down in Uvalde County.
She wrote me this letter, it just came by mail.
She was promised to marry the son of a rich man
She left at the altar in his top hat and tails.

So sing me a song, boys, and saddle my pony,
Send for the foreman and settle my time.
The trail is so long down to Uvalde County;
I'm leaving this life of a cowboy behind.

There's an old country town down in Uvalde County,
A steady job's waiting in dad's general store.
Although I'm a fool for this life I've been living,
You won't see my trails on these ranges no more.

Laurie Wagner Buyer

Cherry Red Winter

Finite questions bring no absolute answers.
The power of mountains stare down daily life.
Caravans of buses streak across the globe.
A microcosm of ocean-blue swamp begs forgiveness.
The emptiness of a dirt track, battered and torn
through a thousand hamlets, disappears against
the smooth skin of broken manzanitas,
the dense trunks scratched past the surface of serenity.
Where was that clean edge of enlightenment?
Nothing else lurks in the broken
dreamland geography of split rocks
except the keen eyes of twelve
fat coyotes staring out of the maze of scrub.
Blobs of dirt and hunks of ash move
between the moon and strong tidal waters.

On a June Afternoon

I sit on the stoop eating fresh fruit:
bananas and strawberries from Mexico,
Anjou pears from Argentina,
oranges from California,
apples from Oregon.

Juicy bites remind me
of someone's skin beneath
my soft, plump lips,
the sharp and sweet sea-like
fragrance of sweat and sex.

Yawning years stretch for breath,
ache for some acknowledgement
other than stripped peels
and awkwardly cut cores
that curl and dry in the sun.

Cotyledon

A slender white arm
rises out of the compost,
like a ballerina in arabesque.

A light green leaf,
still furled and fragile,
reaches for warmth and light.

By morning it no longer matters.
A sequined black ballerina
bows in the first hard frost.

Witness to a Death

A young flicker smashes into the glass
of my narrow sunroom window.

She falls.
A stone to the ground.

Rising from winter weeds
the wind ruffles orange-shafted feathers,

tries to lift her into flight
as I rush to her aid

hold her in my hand:
black speckled breast

bright tangerine blush on cheeks
and nape of broken neck

curved insect-seeking beak
long, thin probing tongue

short, swallow-forked tail
feet clenching empty air

and her limpid liquid eye
reflecting back my own.

Blizzard Night

Sleeping tucked in with sorrow
allows no surface for joy or warmth
only the cold edge of anger caught
in the heavy thigh that presses mine,
the weight of wild worry around
my neck like a millstone so I cannot
float in the wake of my own dreams.

Blown snow borders the window
leaving only a thin oblong opening
through which to see the April night.
The wind argues, past howling,
beyond screaming, whipped now into
beseeching and pleading, so black
with storm even the stars stay dark.

I mean to build a morning fire to erase
the chill of the knife-like kiss
that drove me from the bed, but I am tied
to the thin line of lamp light that splits
the night, revealing a bit of green pushing
up through a brown mat of long dead grass,
reaching for the clean-swept edge of spring.

Five-strand with Stays

The fence trembles when I touch it,
a barrier to bulls, and cows with calves,
to elk that leap over at low spots,
and to antelope that bend ballerina bodies
to slide under, white bellies brushing sage.

I follow suit, buckle at the knees and roll
below the bottom wire, pausing to look up
at barbs bristling with feathery frost
against a sky so blue it bleeds spring,
at strands twisted meticulously by machine.

Snagged tight on the top strand, tufts
of coarse tan hair quiver in the teasing breeze
that rises up from the river, and the stays,
curled like candy canes, wrap around each wire,
thin stiff corsets to keep the fence together.

I could have stayed all day thinking about barbs
and wire and wanting the strong hand of man
to always be this stark and splendid: metal posts
sunk in stony soil, life as delineated and straight
as five strands of steel with close-set stays.

Hay Meadow

willow
wild redtop
river bend
butterfly
shooting star

silver weed
snipe
wooden bridge
foxtail
fringed gentian

aster
ant hill
timothy
alpine pendicularis
elephant heads

queen Anne's lace
deer bed
chamomile
coyote howl
gooseberry

dandelion
muddy ditch
elk track
brome
milk vetch

hawk shadow
water parsnip
rock crossing
magpie
monk's hood

Jon Chandler

On the Rio Grande at South Fork

The lace-thin leather of the boot's sole
succumbs to the erosion of matter,
rending microscopically at the point of greatest pressure
allowing a gap that ruptures further with each step
through gold-flecked gravel
the butter-soft hide from the rump of a bull elk
has long fashioned itself to the foot within
accepting earth and water as protective stains
yet it remains wapiti, wild.

The broad brim of the hat accepts and reflects heat,
fibers shrinking from the early morning shower,
the moisture evaporating in thin, misty trails,
which remold to fit the crown within
while shadowing the countenance below
and aiding eyes that search the pool's surface
absorbing the course of each current and eddy.
The formed felt cloth assists the watery hunt for rising browns
and bestows its spirit, wild.

The track in the soft sand collects water,
the basin displacing a million grains
through delicate pressure of pad and claw.
Oblong, with four parallel scars at its apex
it speaks of a lumbering gait; the river forded.
Elkskin and felt define the man
who kneels at the track,
his thoughts of trout banished,
he extends his hand above the marking
to accept its force, wild.

Texas 1968/1983/1998

Opal—pregnant with Daryl Horn's child
        the night she turned fifteen—
doesn't remember much; a little pain, a little blood,
        the odor of Daryl's old man's English Leather and cigarettes
and the way the shadows cast by headlights played across
        the synthetic fabric of the old Ford's ceiling liner as car after car,
        oblivious to the goings-on shielded by the cottonwoods
        at the far edge of the adjacent wheat field,
        drove down County Road Five and turned at Bender's Corner
toward the fair in Thompson
the same fair Opal attended the following year
        carrying her infant daughter,
only to see Daryl in his crisp uniform hand-in-hand with Carol Anne Conway
two days before he shipped out
disappearing like the ghost he would become in Cambodia.

Opal—arrested by Deputy Sheriff Harold Osborn
the night she turned 30—
doesn't remember much; no real pain, just bad blood,
        the reek of Darlene's boyfriend's beer breath and cigarettes
and the way the shadows cast from the streetlight played across
        the sobbing face of her daughter as car after car,
        oblivious to the goings-on beside the battered mobile home
        set on cinderblocks at the two-mile corner,
        drove down County Road Five past Sanders Bridge
toward the tent revival outside Lawson
the same revival Opal attended the following year
        carrying her infant granddaughter
only to see Darlene hand-in-hand with a boy who thought the baby was her sister
two days before he found out
disappearing like the smoke from an extinguished candle in a sanctuary.

Opal—quiet to her husband Tommy
        the night she turned 45—
doesn't remember much; there was pain, but no blood,
        the aroma from the kitchen at the steak house in Sinclair
and the way the shadows cast by the flickering candle played across
the flocked red wallpaper of the booth as car after car,
oblivious to the goings-on across the scarred pine table
in section four of the Black Angus,
drove down Houston Street to the intersection of Main
toward the dance at the old Cattlemen's Ballroom
the same dance Opal attended the following year
carrying the name of her new husband, John,
only to see Tommy slip a half-pint bottle of Jim Beam
from his boot and pour it down
two days before he cleaned his .44 magnum and made a decision
disappearing like a dream that's only recalled on the cusp of sleep.

The Once-Gangly Kid Looks Back

Standing before the tiny campfire at dawn
shivering from cold and anticipation
the smell of the scratchy wool blanket
inside the flannel cocoon of the sleeping bag,
shielding me from the alpine night,
still encasing me like a scented shroud underneath my heavy jacket
the bacon dancing in the banged-up skillet on an old Coleman stove
aching to take the rod in my hands;
to make the first cast.

Carving her name in an aspen at the river's edge
shivering from longing and uncertainty
the blade of the old Buck knife scarring the white bark
as steel subjugated wood, accepting my crude hieroglyphics
allowing me the secret knowledge that I'd performed an enduring act.
Jim Creek and Patricia, who made me howl at love's merciless moon
aching to take her face in my hands;
to make the first move.

Gripping the scored handle of grandpa's bronzed casket
shivering from grief and belonging
the weight of the thing so dense as I lifted with my brother and cousins
and thought he had been so substantial, and was now merely heavy.
All I envisioned was the creel he'd gruffly presented for my 16th birthday
and the Montana browns and the Wyoming rainbows
and Colorado brookies it had held
aching to take the wicker in my hands;
to make the first remembrance.

Bob Cherry

Collage with Dark Dog

The prism you tie with thread to the kitchen
windowshade is cutglass, a small jewel to separate
the colors of light not yet in our winter sky.

From each side of the table, we taste out morning tea,
wait and watch the dark dog separate itself from blackness,
move into the fresh path where last evening we stopped shoveling.

He pauses, quizzes the sudden wall
of snow where we changed our minds
and went without words to separate beds.

Now I see your early face on mine,
each reflected twice in a doublepaned window
as your spinning bauble facets the collage.

Once now for your side, once then for mine,
Dark-Dog-With-Path
all galleried under a chain-swung light bulb.

Fair Grounds at Fort Worth

Second summer at carnival
and Fred and Sally
and Cal and Alice
and me
all went free to ride and hear the calliope.

And watch ourselves at mirrors.

Watch ourselves warped at mirrors and
ride the carousel up-and-down-and-around.

Alice found the Gypsy mannequin
inside the glass cage where we gathered
to ask the questions and laugh
and watch the light flicker
inside her crystal ball.

And watch robotic hands
jerkstop over her crystal ball.

And watch her mocking mannequin
lips move with
each quarter dropped into the slot
by Fred and Sally
and Cal and Alice.

And me.

We knew the questions before the answers.
And all the answers fit.

Then on to cotton candy and laughter and
ferris wheel and back to the Gypsy
and again the questions and the answers
for Fred and Sally
and Cal and Alice

And me.

But the questions bore the answers.
And all the answers fit.

So on to tunnels with love and
the fat lady and the elephant man
and the barkers with promises of thrills galore
and back to the red-bandannaed Gypsy lady
went Fred and Sally
and Cal and Alice.

And me.

Again we heard the answers that all the questions bore.
And all the answers fit.

   ★ ★ ★

Three summers now and soon
carnival again
and cotton candy
and tunnels with love
and barkers with promises of thrills galore.

And the red bandanna.

And the answers that the questions bear.
But only some of the answers fit.

For Fred and Sally and the Gypsy.

And Alice and me.

Innuendo to a Final Frontier

You see the filching
wolverine but only when your fish are gone –
and still she moves alive behind your eyes,
where she catches for each of your
blurred suspicions of her
a full view of you twice.

You speak to a closing moon
say you know this final phase is not a hole
punched through the blackness of winter sky
by the reckless blade of a miner's spade.

Quasars are far beyond,
there before we named them,
and each star is cold
before its light is ours.

And you know these hollow puddles of wax
in your shallow dish only hint
at whispers from parted lovers
whose candleglow was spent against the darkness.

So you will follow your own break
in the willows,
rest with the reality of a birch at your back,
and like a curve in a river,
define your own embankments
with innuendos in the tremolo of a loon.

Quartet

Two cranes cried outside
the darkened bedroom window last evening,
a tide-filling slough separating
each from each and me from drunken
laughter in the harbor. Fearing night flight

we sought comfort, all in our own music.
Standing barefoot at the curtained window
I furtively parted the folds to listen. Twice more,
breaking from the soft edge of sleep, I returned
once to the late, bold laughter,

once to the fading cries. All
had departed with the morning ebb
and the slick silt on the bank of the slough.
Now each late afternoon, watching the long grass
sink into black water below the embankments

I feel the flood. In solitude,
tuning myself into the swirling twilight
filling the flats between us,
I await the fluid maestro,
the midnight symphony of dissonance.

Two Forces

must have worked on stone shards,
plain and separate halves
from greater rock,
tortured, smoothed, and tumbled
from the cold stream where I wade
like a Sisyphus to his task.

Resting on the other side,
hold the halves in hand,
surveying each,
assessing missing parts,
weigh that force which divides
against that which keeps them so.

Rotating parts to find they fit,
meshing like puzzles,
almost whole,
almost full,
jagged edges a sphere filling
the void inside cupped hands.

A thin and fragile whim
to join the two.
I use a final force—
cold upon the hearth of time—
to turn, toss both,
each half aloft,
each as silhouette
against a mirrored sky,
all pulled as one piece
into the shattered surface
of the stream.

Gaydell Collier

Black Hills Evening

Riding low on the western hills
        the sun throws shadows long
        long to the rising moon
they skip over gullies, slide through treetops
        reaching
        thinning
        stretching

I walk one ridge and watch
        my giant shadow
        walk the next
shadowself embracing
        hawthorns
        snowberry
        lichen-ruffled rocks
        a round-eyed doe

Disappearing into cloud
        as the land dips
        then reappearing
in the evening hush, shadowskin
brushed by cool wind
        and breath of pine
        reaches up to nudge
        the filling moon

then fades
        as the sun
                sinks
                      into
                            the hills.

Scent of Baskets

Grass grows thick at the horseshoe bend
where the creek runs deep
peepers trill
a dragonfly darts in flashes of blue
shadows float upon the water
and root-straggles hang from the cutaway bank
where last year a buffalo skull emerged
in the dark of the turn
ten thousand years old.

Late summer heat presses down from the sun
rises up from grasses, cattails, sedges,
until the scent fills my mind
with out-of-reach longing
gnawing at my memory until
the sun-mist clears
and I am five again
when Woodstock was a village
artists with easels propped in the square
craftsmen with piled wares in front of shops
where I walk hand in hand
with mother and grandmother.

The scent of baskets hanging in the sun.
Dozens of baskets, hundreds of baskets,
not enameled or paint-gaudied,
natural baskets, cottage-woven
plied from reeds and grass.
We carry home a basket
filled with warm sunshine
the scent thick with summer.

How many years
how many miles
to learn that the scent
of eastern baskets
western grasses
and ancient bones
is all the same
drying in the sun?

When the Sodergreen House Burned Down

Unlike modern houses framed with concrete and glass,
This house was hewn from heartwood with a meaning to its past,
When strong men worked with gnarled hands and double-bitted ax
To knit the logs together, dove-tailed, and made to really last –
Made to stand forever, nestled to the land,
Fourteen rooms and hallways fashioned by a settler's hand.

> I've looked from all the windows, walked through all the doors,
> Listened on the strairways, swept the hardwood floors,
> Peered into hidden corners where the joints were fitted well
> Stood out on the back stoop where they rang the dinner bell.

> And I always felt the beat and heard the river flowing
> Out behind the Delco shed where the moss was always growing
> Heard the footsteps of the old times running through the halls
> Felt the warmth and sensed the lifeblood beating in the walls.

There were times when many lived there, times when there were few,
When the rooms were stuffed to bursting with the summer haying crew
Or echoed stark and empty, woodbine shadow-painted floor,
Pet parrots clawed the windowsill, a dog scratched up the door,
Initials carved above the stairs, coins tucked between the beams –
Such a house was made for living, made for laughter, made for dreams.

A house like this was never made to shrivel or to rot
Rafters sagging, vacant windows staring o'er a weed-grown lot.
Better far to reach for glory with a blazing fire out of control
From back steps to second story—burning down its soul
Like a vital bursting artery spewing black smoke to the sky,
A pulsing, ruptured jugular—such a fitting way to die.

Smoldering in the ashes sounds a phoenix-raising cry,
Swells a meaning to the place that will catch you passing by.
You can see it in your mind's eye, step through the spirit door
Climb the spectral staircase, tread the phantom floor,
Peer into the haunted corners where the ghosts of memory glide
And then swirl up around you in an ever-rising tide.

> Hear the footsteps of the old times running through the halls,
> Feel the warmth and sense the lifeblood beating in its walls.
> And always you will feel the beat and hear the river flowing
> Out behind the cottonwoods where the moss is still there growing,

John Duncklee

El Corrido de Antonio Beltran

I listened to the tales of my father
about the days and months
in the land that paid in dollars
the trips north
the bus to the border
the walk along the river
hiding days and walking nights
watching for the *migra*
stopping at ranches and farms
meals for work
sometimes just a meal
Tucson
Phoenix
harvesting the produce from farms
sleeping in shacks or under trees
always on the lookout for the *migra*
green uniforms and green trucks
caught and sent back
only to slip through the fence and return
walking along the river again
going from harvest to harvest
sending money back to Tinaja Verde
and finally home to plant his own field.

Now it was my turn.
Father spent a lifetime in the fields
sitting outside rolling tobacco in a husk
remembering the trails
drawing a map in the dirt with the stick
where to walk
where not to go
friendly ranches

unfriendly ranches
roads
where to find food
dress like a *pocho*
look like you lived in the states
the farmer who didn't pay for two weeks
and when the crop was in
the *migra* came
no pay
he had worked two weeks for nothing
no money to send back to Tinaja Verde.
They tossed pesos in the hat
he would try to repay
but there were no expectations
Rosa with his four
and one in her belly
they would stay to tend the field
wait for money orders at the *correo*
the last night before the bus north
no fears
just a part of life
not poverty
they knew no other way
wealth only a word
not a state of their minds
adios
buena suerte
Tinaja Verde obscured by dust from the bus wheels
towns
cities
tortillas and *frijoles* wrapped in worn cloth
a small amount remaining at the border
enough until he found a ranch by the river
maybe plastic water bottle filled

ready to slip through the fence after dark
head for the river
stay away from railroad crossings
stay away from roads
the *migra* stay in their green cars.

First sunrise
a mesquite *bosque* to hide
last of the *comida*
sleep
awake at the sound of a rattling pickup truck
dirty white not green
a ranch in the distance
friendly one according
to his father's map on the dirt
wait for just before sunset
approach with care
remember the words
food for *comida*
please for *por favor*
thank you for *gracias*
work for *trabajo*
water for *agua*.
No work but a meal
frijoles with some *carne* in a tortilla
enough food for two days
back to the river
north again along a trail
sometimes in the sand
heavy walking
a town with a church
keep going by the moon's light
another *bosque*
hidden for the day

sounds of traffic on the *camino real*
no matter
sleep.
Hot sweat
wet air beneath the trees
sleep again until sunset
awakened by the sound of diesel
eat
back to the river in the dark
wait for the moon
walk walk walk
lights from Tucson getting brighter
under the bridge
more heavy-sand
another bridge
noisy youth drinking beer
"¿*Cerveza?*"
"*No gracias*"
have to reach Mendoza before sunrise
the city asleep
fourth crossing to the right
eight *cuadros*
corner house with name on mailbox
almost sunrise
knock
no matter
early risers
Mendoza comes to the door
"*Sí*, I remember your father"
Spanish is comfortable
coffee brings new vigor
chorizo and eggs fill the void
the cot in the yard
sleep.

Mendoza knows about some work
three days
washing dishes in El Sombrero Café
regular dishwasher gone
Mendoza won't accept dollars for his help
Mendoza knows a man driving to Phoenix
gives me Raider hat to wear
green car parked
ready to chase
the hat fools
safe from Tucson
melons ready to pick outside Phoenix
two weeks
another farm
ten miles to walk
dollars in pocket feel good
ask about *correo* for money order
one hundred bucks to Tinaja Verde.
They say there is work in Idaho
a long way to travel
bus
a chance for the *migra*
always the *migra*.
Fruit to pick
hay to stack
big machines do the grain
farmers glad to have help
pay every week
money orders to Tinaja Verde
how big is Rosa with the new one
how is the field
is father all right
how tall are the children
some *amigos* plan for California

good money but lots of *migra*
some say best to find *migra* in Idaho
free trip back to border
free *comida*.
California by bus
lucky no *migra*
plenty of work
grapes
thousands of *toneladas*
the vines hide us from the *migra*
more money orders to Tinaja Verde
six months
I wonder about Rosa
the new one should be born soon
boy or girl
maybe a boy to help in the field
I will draw a map in the dirt when he is ready
time to think about going back
two more weeks in the grape vines
farmer asks me to stay for planting
steady work
I say I will come back in a month
I must see Rosa
the children
the new one
I want to see the field.
The farmer says stay
I want to stay for the dollars
there are other farmers
there will be work again in a month
I say *gracias*
adios.

The highway
no *migra*
Raider hat in back pocket
straw hat for the *migra*
a ride to the border
no *migra*
a *policia* stops
asks questions
he talks on his radio to *migra*
bueno
a free ride to the border.
Mexicali
big city
first two nights in jail at the *migra* office
thirty of us
loaded into bus like cattle
some did not get far from Mexicali
dollars inside shoes
unload from bus like cattle
through the gate
Mexico
bus to Sonora
south from Santa Ana
Tinaja Verde through the windshield
the bus stops just for Antonio Beltran
I walk to the house by my field
Rosa hands me our new son.
After *comida*
I take the old guitar from the wall
I begin playing
singing a new song
El Corrido de Antonio Beltran.

In the Corner

In the corner of the corrugated shed
an old saddle, unnoticed,
half hidden by a layer of gray-brown dust.

A pair of chaps, cracked and scraped,
hanging from a horn burned and grooved by dallies,
saddle strings stretched and hard.

By the door on a wooden rack
another saddle tooled with distinct design –
the smell of oil, new-tanned leather.

For months, mile after mile, it will squeak.
Perhaps in fifty years it will earn its wear,
its smell, its dust, in the corner.

Dan Guenther

About Elk

At twilight the Evergreen herd
lingered at the Genessee exit for over an hour,
gazing upon the highway
and the first of the emerging stars.

Blinded by the oncoming headlights,
they turned and moved eastward,
the setting sun at their backs,
restless with the memory of journeys
never completed, of paths not taken.

Once they migrated great distances
across the plains
to find refuge in the high country, always
at one with the blue mountain's backbone.

Now they wait for the season's change to tie
together the whole,
resting at the edge of the sheltering trees,
deep into their premonitions,
like so many dark haystacks.

Hunter

He stops the car to listen
to what drops out of the wind.

Cries within the pines lift his spirits,
the search for the sudden and unforeseen,
continuous, even in his dreams.

The longings of this hunter
connect with the seamless net of time,
to landscapes resonating with the meditations
of locusts, to the languorous eyes of mule deer.

The dark has always been his smooth companion.

Many a night along the river bank
he turns circles in the tall grass to make a bed.

Keeper of the Ute's Winter Moon

In the early light
mares guide their colts down Bear Creek,
along a trail once used by the Mountain Utes.

After a sleepless November night
subtle ghosts settle with the first snow on the foothills,
and the cry of a lynx freezes the lead mare.

Searching among the dry leaves of the scrub oaks,
she expects to find yellow eyes gazing back;

Or perhaps spirits of the long dead
rattling their hidden rabbit bones,
while cottonwoods shed golden leaves
to the silent flight of an owl.

A glimpse among a stand of spruce
sees a silver shadow slipping away to the west,
beneath the setting winter moon.

When deer move down the mountain

Tempted to board a bus for Mexico,
the last cowboys howl and yip at the Morrison Cantina.

The cold coming in
has all wild things on the move,
the natural order turning around,
coyotes prowling roadside ditches,
a cougar digging up old graves south of Littleton.

The high country exiles, both the gorgeous and profane,
head down the mountain, following the deer.

When the rattlesnakes retreat from their broad, flat rocks
to tangle together,
we transcend our separateness in the lull of the afternoon,
listening through the silences,
wrapping together for warmth.

Linda Hussa

The Un-doing of Heaven's Match

She's returning books
borrowed against the echo of an empty house.
Never read them, I bet. Doesn't
taste the coffee I set before her,
doesn't feel the pick-me-up of its intention.
So deep in the blues.

Husband's gone from a marriage
that took her
from one end of her thirties to the other.

It's suppertime. She says, *Can't stay.*
Red silk blouse says
she's on the hunt of something in town.
But no good time will get close
without a collision on the sorrow she wears.

Grew up on ranch, married a rancher.
A team going from dark to dark
building a place. We saw it, the way neighbors do
when there's miles and miles of work between you.

At brandings they snaked calves from the bunch –
careful but fast—God's gift
and purely loving to rope. Head catch
with an ocean wave, heel with a backhand
over the hip, a yip and a yowl!
The ground crews timed their look-ups
just to see their dancing loops.

They lived close in a casual way.
Both wore the grease, both wore pants.

When it came apart
it was like trying to bale feathers –
no way to gather it up.

He was there for the work,
but he'd found himself a towngirl
with polish on her nails and time on her hands.

She lifted her cup and asked the cold coffee,
Wasn't I woman enough for him
or wasn't I enough of a man?

Basque Herders

Desert bands always on the move.
Bedroll on new ground each night.
Aspen leaves tremble,
Afraid of the darkness beyond the fire.

He carves tree after tree
—name and year.
How long did he promise to stay?
Hands over the smooth bark
thinking—woman
hearing—the ridicule of the raven.

On Sunday he sets his own altar.
His home village is bread and wine.

The camptender brings supplies, news,
And takes away
His folded words that speak to home,
I am still here, and
I am still there with you.

January Gift

Alone chopping the evening's wood
I bend to gather up kindling
and chance to see
a cloud taking up half the sky.

Folded layers of yesterday's blood
and the white-hot light of Heaven
are a swan floating on the endless blue.
I call for someone, anyone,
to come see. There is no one in earshot.

Only the old dog, blind in one eye,
dragging a cow leg up from the creek.
Obedient, he comes, drops the bone,
sits at my feet.
I turn his good eye toward the cloud.
His breath stinks of life in transition.

I watch the cloud until it fades
into many shades of darkness coming on.
I memorize the cloud.
When I need it most, color and shape
will be resurrected.

The dog buries his bone
with the same sense of duty.

W.C. Jameson

The Air

It changed the moment I stepped onto the southern bank
after crossing the Rio Grande del Norte.

The air in Mexico is different from the air in Texas.
The pungency of dense creosote bush assails the nostrils,
but it took only moments to grow accustomed to it,
to like it.

But there was more, much more
to the Mexico air.

Sometimes it moved calmly,
sometimes violently,
but always with an underlying urgency.

It was crisp, most often clean
unless, in the movement,
delivering a load of dust and sand.
Its Chihuahuan and Sonoran dryness robbed the moisture
from the ground, the streams,
the soil, the trees, the brush.

Sometimes it carried the smell of animals,
alive and dead.
Sometimes it carried the smell of men,
alive and dead.

When one lives in the desert for a long time
one can detect the difference
in the smells of love and fear,
both of which are carried on the Mexico air.

And always, always,
the air,
whether advecting across the sandy desert surface
or dancing softly through a glade,
carries the smell of danger.

The Headstone

A simple marker
Seven steps from the trail.
Old sandstone, badly weathered.
The inscription barely readable:

>Porfirio Lucero
>Born Nov. 1945   Died Aug. 1958
>Killed by his father

Back to the wind, collar up,
Hat pulled down low and tight,
Chilled hands deep in pockets,
The silica sound
Of saltating grains of sand
Strike the stone
Near my feet.

To Beat the Devil

In the cantinas of Colima
we wasted days and surrendered nights
while searching for love and enlightenment,
while searching for meaning, searching for life.

But you can't find the truth in tequila or maidens,
or maybe you can
when you're chasing it down with a passion
in a place where you've never been.

In the taverns of Tepehuanes we bloodied our fists
on the faces of fortune and smashed them to bits.
We counted our winnings and found we had lost,
we considered our options, confused at the cost.

We were just trying to beat the devil
and sing our own songs,
but the reasons had no rhyme
and the words came out all wrong.

So, we kicked in the doors
and learned some new parts;
we went for their throats,
and tore out their hearts.

Los Zopilotes

We had ridden over a mile from the battlefield,
heartbeats and breath only just beginning to slow.
Sweat streamed down faces, arms, legs, torsos,
clothes smelled like gunsmoke,
bodies atremble with victory,

As we rode Indian-file toward the east
I turned in the saddle
and looked back down the trail
beyond the low ridge we just crossed
and watched a plume of smoke rising
and drifting toward us
high in the sky, blown by the west wind.

Detecting a dark, silent movement
I glanced up
and spotted *el zopilote*
gliding in wide circles above the smoke.
Soon he is joined by another,
and another,
until there are dozens of the black vultures
circling, descending in an ever-tightening spiral
toward the dead,
eight of them, lying where they fell in the sand,
lying in pools of their own blood.

This evening *los zopilotes* will feast
but we will not.
We ride to the next battle.
We ride to forget the last.

So Much Time Has Passed

On my last trip to the foothills of the Sierras
in the Chihuahuan countryside
I learned they were all gone.

Borrego was captured and hung by the *vaqueros*.
Sanchez was shot by a firing squad.
Candelaria was crucified
along the road to Boquillas.
Paco was beheaded.
Chavez disappeared.

I found old Jaramillo
in the jail at Camargo.
They made him mop the stones
and concrete
every day.
They cut out one of his eyes
with the heated tip of a knife.

I went to see him.
They made me wait for two days.
When they finally let me in
Jaramillo gripped me tightly,
hugged me long.
We both wept.

Celinda Kaelin

Custer's Boots

"May we know his heart,
so that the People will live."

Golden flakes of tobacco
tumbled into the pipe's bowl with
these words as the People prepared to send
a voice to the Creator.

Solemn faces watched spirals of smoke rise.
But the smoke was black. Not silver.

The warrior's heart did show itself.
So the ashes of his thoughts, returned to their rightful owner,
were dumped on his boots.

Golden light spilled across a gentle
mound crowned with slender stalks
of buffalo grass bunched in tight camp
circles which caught, held, reflected back
the cloying glow of late sun.

Crimson streamed through
silky strands of yellow hair,
found its way onto the fringes
of the fallen warrior's leather shirt.

Lifeless, lead-colored, like
a ribbon of melted bullets,
concrete threads its way
through the buffalo grass
to the stone, two ponies high,
placed by his people
where the warrior's Spirit took its walk.

Hard and sharp,
like the point of a war lance,
the obelisk thrusts upward.
Piercing
Breast of Mother Earth
Piercing
Heart of Father Sky.

Do his people understand
The power of the Pipe after all?

Holy Woman Tree

I pause and glance over my shoulder, watching the sun climb over
        the great peak.
Inch by inch, he pierces her darkest crevices with lances of pure buffalo light.
I hold my palms upward, toward my Father, welcoming his Spirit into mine.
Renewed, I now continue after my pony, tracking him
across the meadow and along a trace carved into the blushing
granite by thousands of lodge poles trailing behind prancing Indian ponies.
Velvet-swirled branches of sage bathe my moccasins
in pungent unction with each step,
blessing my errand at this sacred time, when darkest night meets rose light.

Crisp, dew-heavy air fills my lungs as I hasten into the needled embrace
        of the pines.
As these massive Standing Ones close around me, I see her.

She stands, twisted and gnarled, an aged Ponderosa Pine
bearing the marks of four ropes where they vainly sought to hold her
close to the ground when she was a sapling.
These four, finger-wide grooves mark the first turn of her trunk,
while a medicine scar the length of my arm climbs along below.
High above, naked branches intermingle with hoary green,
bearing witness to her purification by the Thunder Beings.

Holding a pinch of tobacco between left thumb and forefinger,
I raise my hand to the Grandfathers and Grandmothers of the
West, North, East, and South.
Closing my eyes, I then crumble this sacred herb along her ancient wound.
Overhead, the Spotted Eagle calls.

Now, I see her as she appeared in my dream.
She stood at this spot, in the lingering clouds of dust
from her traveling village just beyond the hill.
She stood, unmoving, beside her travois—watching my approach.

A gentle breeze fingered the snow-white fringes of her buckskin dress,
while her large doe eyes held my gaze under a brow framed by obsidian hair.

I momentarily broke the bondage of her stare, and gaped at the bundle
tied to the lodge poles wedged on each side of her pony.
Heavy with its burden, the buffalo robe was swollen to its gather,
spilling golden flakes, like dust mites in the sunlight,
    from its overflowing corners.

When I turned again to my benefactress, she pointed at the travois
    with her chin.
"Use this for the People."

Sundancing at Pine Ridge

"A serpent is in your midst!"

Sun Dance Chief heeds rattler's warning,
honors this messenger with painless death.
Lifeless,
rattlesnake now lies coiled in the earth,
high on a hill where
undulating veils of heat
carry his spirit upward.
I crumble tobacco on his grave,
"Thank you."

Below, pine bough arbor embraces dance circle.
At center, forked cottonwood shakes branches,
cavorts with Wind, flashes banners.
These Medicine colors—black, white, red, and yellow –
call the Winged Ones,
each Feathered a herald for Creator:
Owl foretells death;
Butterfly mirrors transformation;
King Bird warns of enemies;
Eagle signals work well done.

At shrill call from eagle bone whistle,
eighty dancers file into Mystery Circle.
First, men.
Their red kilts, edged with Medicine colors,
vibrant as buffalo blood.
Next, women.
Long cotton gowns, rainbows of color,
sleeves flapping like butterflies.
All wear crowns of sage.
All wear wrist bands of sage.

"Whoosh!"
Black and white Wingeds flush overhead
as sisters, daughters, mothers, grandmothers enter.

Roiling above shade arbor, these King Birds call our gaze,
then rush into outstretched arms of Cottonwood.
Creator has now warned twice.

Four red days, four blue days,
round and round Sundance Tree
first light to black night.
Rumbling thunder,
drum's voice,
rolls through Mystery Circle
sending wave after wave
through moccasins,
up legs,
clutching belly
until heart pounds in unison.

Memories of clear, cold, sweet water
torture mouth.
Bite hard on bitter bear medicine,
"Grandfather, have pity!"
Knees wobble, vision full of black spots,
body struggles to stand, to dance.
Breathe sweet scent of cedar smoke,
"Grandfather, have pity!"

Testing hearts, Father Sun
transforms earth to oven.
Slender stalks of grass, seared brown,
stab soles with each step.
Leathery lungs labor to lead feet
across parboiled pebbles.
At last, Sweat Lodge calls.

Blistering vapors from stone cool sizzling breath of Sun
till I have no more sweat to give.
But in the Lodge and throughout the days
I hear harsh words from one in turquoise kilt.
Then I hear Grandfather;
"Tell him 'Thank you.'
Don't let him sew black threads of anger.
Don't allow his arrow words to wound."

"But, Grandfather, this man is *Heyoka*;
has dreamed of Thunder Beings.
Dances Kettle Dance, assists Sun Dance chief,
carries power of black and white dog.
Why do the colors of his skirt echo the colors of my shawl?"
My heart opens, and I hear Grandfather again.
"Dance hard, Wolf Woman!
Dance hard, for the children."
I focus tear-filled eyes on chokecherry bundle
cradled in forked branches of *Wagachum* and obey.

Fourth day!
"Thank you, Grandfather."
In dusky light of approaching night,
Body electric with love and gratitude,
I leave Mystery Circle embraced by Spirit and ancestors.
As we exit west doorway—Turquoise Kilt.
I shake his hand. Search his face for understanding.
But he has no eyes.
Only sockets filled with amber glow.

* * *

In vision, Black Elk, Lakota holy man,
saw these times.
Warriors, coming from Pike's Peak,

doing battle with black and white dog.
A spiritual battlefield for two-leggeds;
a flipping from hate to love.

Amber eyes haunt me.
I want to erase them from my mind,
cleanse their memory from my pores,
flush them in droplets from my body,
wash them into Mother Earth.
At Sweat Lodge, thunder bug comes,
so tiny that I almost miss him but for his
"Click, click, click"
as he flips over and over.

Page Lambert

Culling Buffalo at Yellowstone

In a darkened conference center
across a square-cornered video screen
shadowed images of starving buffalo wander
wading through the snow of diseased winters.

At the far end of my table
a Lakota girl plays with a small rubber ball
molded and colored to look like the earth.
Her toy escapes, rolls down the length
of stark white tablecloth.

My ball! she calls—
I roll the rounded earth back
closing the distance
watching green continents turn upside-down,
blue oceans spilling still water.

Thank you, she whispers—
the dim room gravid with ghosts
dead these three hundred years
these three days, three hours, three minutes.

I pray the girl does not hear
the narrator's voice slice the silence:
Regardless of the results of the brucellosis test
all pregnant females will be put down.

Dispersal

Alone, after fifteen spring calving seasons,
twenty-four married winters,
I step out the barn door,
pieces of alfalfa cake in my pockets,
specks of manure on my boots.

I said I would not grieve
but I am crying and cannot stop.
"It's hard," is all he said
as he left for the sale barn
with the first trailer load of cows.

Bittersweet, being so at home
here, among coiled bridles and calico cats,
the next load of mothers mulling in the corral,
breathing hay and grain and grass,
watching slow dust rise from horse hooves.

In the sun, I sit in the shadowed aspects of my life.
A bridge could have been built
were it not for the silence, both of ours,
the mountain could have been climbed if only we'd
taken small Sherpa steps, felt the resilient earth
accommodate both our journeys.

Even as the Antler

Listen for the sound
of one tree cradling another
the creak of limb, the moaning of wind
silent deadfall on the forest floor.
Even elk must sometimes choose
to walk divergent paths.

His tracks leave hers
move out from beneath boughs
hanging too thick
for rub or rattle
move beyond the swirls of grass
that mark the night bed of cow and calf.

Kneel on the trodden mat
breathe lingering warmth
smell folded legs
split hooves, rounded belly
inhale the grazed breath of autumn
hear the ghost of whispered mews.

It's all a dance, I am discovering
a woodsy waltz
a celebration rising
always rising
even as the antler sheds
even as the cradled tree falls.

Max McCoy

Summer is short and the night is long

I

So I walk the river road at night,
sit by the water beneath stars,
watch the moon rise over pools,
feel the tide within my veins and dare
to drink the mystery of her again.

How many times? A thousand, no less,
each but a part of one long night
sustained by memory though
no hope of dawn is in sight.

I could curse whatever I must have done
but the wind stirs the river, the voice of sorrow.
The night pleads, tell me the story,
the pain of dreams and desires.

Draw close, I say, comfort me
and I'll spin you the tale of darkness,
the chill that makes me seek the flame,
the warm embrace of those who are blessed
with eternal day, those who, blind from birth
by the beauty of the light, are damned to forget its worth.

Better one summer of love and not forget
than to share a lifetime and remember nothing.
Like roses gathered in the spring
these things cannot be held for long,
they fade and hands grow weak
as the paradox grows stronger.

Words are but light from distant fires.
Mere pen and paper have no power
except that which is granted by desire,
the words of one writer who loved
and did not forget.

When she comes to me again,
I will lead her to the water's edge,
drink the mystery once more,
lie with her, meet the tides' demand.
I will fight the fear of both hand and flower,
touch her cheek, burn away the hours.

II

so I went to the hospital,
said, "I'm discontinuing treatment
for an unequivocal lack of results
and I want my books back
especially that $75 text written
by the woman at John Hopkins
who never answered my letters.

But I can't blame her
she must be busy
suffers from manic depression too.
Oh, sorry, it's bipolar now,
but that's too nice a word
for something that kills one in five,
besides, who the hell am I?"

The receptionist smiles,
dials a secret number.

Sad Edgar Allen Poe stares at me
from a drug company poster.
"At your age," old Edgar says,
"I was dead. Still, I'm not forgotten.
Your life, however, has neither rhyme nor meter."

The titles of his most famous work float
around his head. What is he trying to say?
That it's better to hide in a chemical fog
or forego surcease and feed this fever?

The receptionist surrenders the phone.
I hear the doctor's voice through the cellular noise:
"We need to talk. Can you come at five?"

"I prefer not," I say, my reply thick with Melville.
"Thanks for the help, but after eight years
I'm tired of the pain. It's not your fault I'm quitting.
So long."

I hand the phone back, smiling.
The elevator takes forever to come
and in that eternity I ponder how to do it:
a gun, probably the shotgun dad left me.
A single round of double-ought buck.

I begin to cry as the door slides open
to take me down to my 25-year-old
pickup with boxes of books in the bed,
remainders, mostly, obscure titles
of unequal length, and on the cover of each
a name no one will remember.

III

so I walk into the Farmers and Drovers Loan
say, "Get down or I'll blow your heads off,
this isn't as easy as it looks, I'm wound
tighter than piano wire and my heart's
hammering a Steve Earle song ...

What the hell did I tell you?
Hug the ground!
This 870 Remington
with the sawed-down barrel
will blow a hole in you
the size of a basketball.

Be quick.
Fill that sack.
No alarms or dye packs.
No time to fuck around.
The clock's ticking.
My life's counting down
in minutes and seconds.

All I ever wanted
was to feed my kids and make
the payments on the truck
but then I got laid off at the bacon plant
and the old lady left me. . . .
Been looking for a job so long
can't even call myself unemployed.
All the benefits run out –
something inside finally broke
and I don't know which way to turn.

I never had nothing I didn't lose.
Never did nothing but get high.
Never got a chance to really live...

wish I could tell the kids I love them
but I'd never say I was sorry.

Okay,
a million cops outside,
go on, all of you, get out,
I'd rather die in this damned bank
than get shot from behind
by somebody I trusted
because I know how that feels:
love is hard, like a bullet."

Red Shuttleworth

Lyndon Baines Johnson (1928)

Cadaver-thin, he stalks up the tracks
out of Cotulla, Texas. The tickle in his throat
gives way to the first whiskey in weeks.
At twenty he is scarcely older than his seventh grade
Mexican students at Wellhaven Elementary School,
still blurts, too obviously goggles married women,
compulsively smokes, and damned well can't sleep.
At the edge of town, he bellows at the north wind,
"My students will be stamped with learning,
will not be subdued. By God they will cut loose,
immortal, and grow to love goodness, without hunger."
Then, in darkness, he mocks himself, says, "Shit."
He winces at his own rhetoric, yet prays on his knees
to be sent on a terrible journey worth caring about.

Elman Card (1937)

"What kind of life can you have
if over three hundred boys and girls died
when the school blew up while you played hooky?
I was home, rubbing my arm with Absorbine,
which also kills ringworm of the foot,
home, not a half a mile away, thinking,
how my speedball leaves an exhaust trail,
thinking I'm the new Dizzy Dean. Then . . . Boom.
Air waves take out my bedroom window. Sister's body,
skin aged to silvery blue, is in the rubble.
Ma and Pa gulp whiskey, lie to each other that sister
is at Bible camp. What kind of life is there,
nuts to baseball, if shame and guilt
burn us from New London to Dallas?"

John Wilkes Booth (1938)

"Between Post and Clairemont there are,
for one particular mile, as many fence posts
as there are skinned wolves dangling off them,
over two hundred nearly identical grimaces.
I am no more Lincoln's assassin than you, friend,
but you have paid your twenty-five cents to leer
at my arsenic-embalmed black flesh, to peek
up my khaki shorts, to ruffle my white hair.
I am John St. Helen from Enid, Oklahoma,
a lovesick suicide stuffed with straw.
My left leg is shorter, thus I am Booth?
I swallowed a B-engraved pendant for jealousy's
white flame, so I am Booth? But shake my hand,
place my palm upon your true love's breast."

Huron "Ted" Waters (1938)

"I never said I was some trigger-quick,
matchless Lucky Luciano, Al Capone, or Dillinger.
You got to go a caliber extra in the crime shindig
to be Clyde Barrow or Miss Bonnie Parker,
but you can tell folks I pitched pennies
with them. I have a talent for stealing
hens and eggs, for driving Cadillacs, and once rode
steers at rodeos as far north as Burwell, Nebraska.
I'm a common, decent Texas boy, though my looks
are swank enough for Hollywood, wild sure,
but until I met Clyde, my most daring adventure
was running around on Halloween, tipping over outhouses.
I'm in the Dallas jail thanks to Mr. Hoover, making me
Public Enemy Number One, your essential R.C. Cola thief."

Milton Parker Looney (1994)

"Light 'em if you have 'em": the fighting Nora's
Navy Cross fire controlman is dying, lung cancer,
hot as the Christmas lights as his niece's house.
In delirium he is back on the Northampton,
just before midnight near Guadalcanal
at a surprise party for a convoy of Jap destroyers.
He's having a smoke with radioman Jason Robards,
balancing future fame and California redheads,
talking Texas horses and Galveston weekends.
Bam-Bam. A pair of torpedoes hit the port side.
Flaming diesel fuel sprays across the Northampton.
Boxed ammo explodes, rips into his side as he shoots
a rope gun at the mast to rescue a man. He is nudged
awake by his pastor, teeth white as cigarette paper.

George Sibley

Hartman Rocks

I lift my eyes to these hills
To see beyond gods and folly;
I come out among these rocks
To take peace in their absence of plan.

In this thrust and boil of stone,
Long cooled but still settling out,
The penetrant thrust and twist of root
Sorting mineral from dust beneath sun,
The dry vagrant prowl of insistent air
And a tree's gnarled hope for rain:
In this mishmash of eternal fiddling
I finally come free of God, destiny: free.

Philosophers ask what life means, or meant;
The rocks make me believe: accident.
In the beginning was no word, just swirl
And press of rampant roiling energy
Rearranging itself in random shots
Even more solid and slow till this latest form,
This long drawn death in beauty and brokenness
In the rocks that rise in ruin all around.

The word, if it comes at all, is dragged here
By such as me: a buzzing busyness at surface
That interrupts the bright waiting silence
Not at all, or not enough to matter.

Hawks and Haying at Clarke's Ranch

They seemed a team, symbiotic:
The silent man on the John Deere,
The hawk floating along behind,
Waiting for something to dart out
Of the over-rolled row of winnowed hay.

With my English major's romantic camera
I put together the pictures and poetry
That showed up in that week's paper.
Clarke chuckled. "You ever buck a day of bales,
You'll see some different pictures."

Next year Clarke was gone, forever.
But I was there again, helping his sons buck the bales.
He was right. Finally they put me up on the wagon;
Arms and knee could no longer boost from the ground
So I just shuffled the bales into place.

Braced against the lurching hay, sweat and bugs
In my eyes nose and crotch, I laughed along
With the kind jokes, kinder than sympathy,
About my puny arms, fit only for typing and beer-bucking —
And glancing up, saw the winglocked hawk loft above us.

Just the hawk, left from last year's team,
Floating over the draw where I'd followed the tractor,
An abrupt upthermal carrying her
Aslant beyond the aspeny slopes and
On above Round Mountain into the cirrus rivers
Of the sky where she hovered and gyred
And whatever had ever been together there
Felt as together as ever.

On Driving Past the One Hundred Thousandth Roadkill

These animals sleeping on the shoulder
Will one day all wake up and take back the roads.
The fish flushed in turbines will run
Up the rubble of dams coming down;
New feathers will grow through crude gunk
And a million white birds will take back the air.

And from that end of our dull oppression of excess,
Our double-entry simplism of borrowing the future
To pour down the bottomless black hole of the present:
Seeing that happen
Some more beautiful thing may even emerge from us;
Something capable of sitting still,
Reinventing the art of growing quiet,
The unimaginable emptying of mind for
The prowlthrough and indwell of the whole ray of life,
The inflight and upwheel of those reborn birds
Sweeping us up into what could be—this could be.

West Elks Haiku

—*For Grant Ferrier*

the old deacon spruce
stood grim but its new greens laughed
as they slapped me wet

that clawed-up quakie's
so old even her bear is
some fifty yards dead

aspens in the pond
shimmer off—don't know down like
the real ones know up

this tall quiet place
was the library when all
the books were still trees

up in these meadows
it's the ants, not the mountains
that make me feel small

to get a life go
into the woods and look for
the map of a tree

Larry D. Thomas

Blue Norther

When the wind barreled in,
even the mesquite murmured,
their roots of tempered steel creaking,
clawing deep in the merciless Texas earth,
their wood ornery enough

to ruin the teeth of chain saws.
Everything in the pasture
groaned under a terrible burden
of ice: the prickly pear, the stock tank,
the rocks, even the cracked dirt itself.

I didn't realize how frigid it was
until I saw the hawk,
beak half-open in an utterance
locked in bubbles of bloody ice,
upright body claw-clung atop

the cedar post of a barbed wire fence,
pointed due north like the wrought
iron cock of a weather vane,
that winter morning of a record low
colder than the bones of the dead.

Forgotten Horseshoe

In far West Texas,
foundationed on a flank
of the Guadalupe Mountains,
just the weathered
wooden shell of Williams Ranch.

A hundred yards from the ranch house,
I find a horseshoe anchored upright,
half-buried in sun-baked earth,
wreathed by a strand of barbed wire,
a relic of the century's turn,

covered with a fuzz of rust
yet stubbornly intact,
forged in the late eighteen-hundreds
of iron and fire.
Though razed by bleak decades

of rasping wind, it never bends,
latching earth to firmament,
quaking forever after
with the murderous hoof
of a piebald stud.

Near Pecos

The land brown with drought,
branches of mesquite
twist to the breaking point.

Fresh brands fester, itching
the hides of Herefords
whose bawling singes hairs

in the ears of cowhands
crossing boots on porch rails,
facing west, their Stetsons

pulled down, singed eyes
dazzled with the hellfire
of sundown's red-orange,

leathery, dust-caked
eyelids the only shades
they lower for the night.

Night Goat

The cold rock faces
of sheer cliffs shudder,
echoing the black
arpeggios of bleating.

He swaggers up the steep
canyon as if he owns
the place, crumbling clods
in the vises of cloven

hooves, clanging
against walls of iron
the clapper of his bell.
He struts, staring

into moonlit firmament,
his agate eyes blazing,
ricocheting the lightning
bolts of starlight.

Sierra Diablo

Near Van Horn, Texas,
in the desert,
even the living is far
more skeleton than flesh;
a landscape of yucca

flanking rib cages
sandblasted, sun-bleached,
immaculate; arroyos
where remnants of the dead
denied decent burial

by the wind
have given themselves up
to nothing but sun and moon;
draws where pelvises
loom shrinelike

and skulls are nothing
but blanched, eternal
offerings of white prayer
to mountains of bleakness
blessed with the name *Diablo*.

Mark Todd

Mountain Roads

The roads I like best
struggle to bridge two points
strung out rubber thin,
like a hat ear to ear,
its band tearing free
from a warped-fitting brim.

Good roads rattle time
with washboard rock-hard ruts,
tire-chewing the day's pace
to no more than a walk,
stretching distance the same
as any stretch of miles.

A proper road resists
travel for the end's sake,
feral, like mountain trails
that vanish beneath my feet,
make me search the land's lay
as I stride ground with care.

Careful journeyed roads
can draw in my thoughts,
stumble-honest and fixed
on what lies, not there, but here
on the next-lurch grade ahead.
Roads worth the trek.

Like Sleep, But Brittle

Like sleep. But brittle,
a film that crackles
from each toss to turn
and then returns
to the starch of wakefulness.

And still the moon stalks
across the floor, its snarl
a predation of light
ready to sink shafts of claw
into sleeping wood.

My shallow breaths
pull at the hours, each a gate
of brass and hinged shadow
that will not open
until the knock of time.

But a cat purrs warmth
into my back, kneads the ridges
of my spine with soft throbs,
as I drift, unaware,
on the margins of a thin night.

Runaway

well I'd unhooked the trailer
just like I'd done a hundred times
I chocked the wheels
I set the block and cranked
it off the hitch

so maybe it
did wobble just a bit, but still
just like I'd done before
then drove off down the slope

that's when my wife dropped
her pitchfork and ran
right past the truck
waving her hands in the air
while the trailer aimed at two yearlings
watching from the fence's other side

there she was, just a little thing
but running to meet that thousand pounds
of trailer speeding down the hill
like her hundred pounds
and swinging hands could stop
its down-hill speed
like it would take one look at her
and say, huh, and come to a halt

all the while, I looked on
and the yearlings looked on
watching her meet
the trailer meeting her
and all of us wondering
what would happen next

before I knew, I was backing
our one-ton truck
to block the trailer's roll

just in case my wife's hands failed

and trying to decide if those yearlings
would move before the trailer hit
the fence and how much it would cost
to fix the truck when a thousand pounds
of steel smacked hard into the bed

still rolling in reverse
my wife jumping to the side
yearlings not moving a step
the truck still easing back

and then the trailer lurched
against a narrow rut
of borrow ditch and smacked
the hitch against the fender skirt
just as the trailer's wheels
bounced quick and ripped a tire
wide open as everything stopped
on top of the road

those yearlings standing
looking at the trailer
just in front of them

wife-truck-yearlings all okay

with just a fender dent
and ruined tire to show
how fast my heart was beating

Lori Van Pelt

Snowy Range Moon

In dusk's chiaroscuro
while sunset drains the day's warmth
we sip burgundy from crystal.

Clad in down coats and wool socks,
we wobble in lawn chairs on cushiony grass
and watch constellations uncloak.

In the clamorous quiet
croaking frogs orchestrate a concerto
night hawks mimic war whoops
coyotes chant canyon cantatas.

While we breath intense air
the luminous appearance
of the bulbous moon diffuses
gleaming beams on sharp peaks.

Tardy Visitor to the Graveyard

Two cocoons dangle
from one budded branch
of the Russian olive.

Little lanterns yet unlit
waiting for luminescence
kindled by interior instinct.

Silken envelopes encase
tenuous gossamer wings –
the power of butterflies.

Near the bunched willows
two blue herons rise
from the warm spring
carrying small trout
into quiescent air.

Trumpeting conversation
as only mates do
Canadian geese circle
wings pumping
whisking April air
into a downy breeze
drawing a crazy figure eight
in the chill dawn sky.

Coasting over crisp cottonwoods
past the double rectangle stone
the heart-beat of paired wings
unbound by mortal restrictions
glorifies the fragile sunrise.

The Deaf Lady Sings

Her garden delights the eyes –
cosmos, roses, irises swinging
in the brisk rhythmic wind
lilacs, poppies, tulips tapping
white wooden picket fence.

In her yard's carnival of color
flowers harmonize,
crescendo to exuberant forte.

She cannot hear the robin
chirping in the marble birdbath
nor pianissimo of feathers...

but the deaf lady sings through her flowers.

Dale L. Walker

Eldorado

Rough and ready, serenely isolated
among pines and oaks and blackberry brambles,
the archetypal placer camp
where the mind still sees weary men stirring
from their bedrolls at daybreak,
cooking coffee, bacon, beans;
where pick and shovel noises mingle with the chatter
of miners digging coyote holes,
hammering up rocker, Long Toms, flumes;
where at night canvas walls glow in orange lantern light,
where a tent saloon crowns with noisy revelers
placing pinches of precious dust on the table
and calling for the turn of a card.

So many of the old gold camps shouldering
the Sierra foothills are buried under reservoirs,
man-made lakes, and the seas of mud,
but some have survived: pastoral villages,
a few thriving towns, persistent placer
and quartz gold camps framed by old stands
of ponderosa and digger pines, groves of oaks
and shag-barked madrones, broad-leafed maples,
and red-stemmed manzanita shrubs abuzz
with bees and shimmering with butterflies,
where golden meadows are cleft by rivers,
streams, arroyos, dizzying mountain trails,
and the granite spires of the Sierra Nevada.

A half-mile west of Fippins' Blacksmith Shop
in Rough and Ready a rutty road called Stagecoach Way
leads to the summit of a sun-bleached hilltop
and a graveyard-full of unvisited, weed-invaded plots
marked by old headstones, homemade, odd-shaped,
hand-chiseled and so eroded by the elements
that most of the legends on them have vanished
as utterly as those lying beneath them,
the words on a few made legible
by rubbing them with a damp cloth.

One reads

> *John A. Smith*
> *Born June 24, 1826, Fairfax County, Va.*
> *Emigrated to Missouri in 1839*
> *And in 1849 to California where he dies June 5, 1863*
> *Peace be to his ashes*

All of the gold country—every crossroad,
rivulet, copse of trees, and wildflowered hillside—
is animated by the ghosts of the John Smiths,
the dauntless gold hunters who came here from faraway places
like Massachusetts, Sonora, Pernambuco, Canton,
Marseilles, Sydney, Manila, the Sandwich Islands,
and none of those who followed the argonaut trails—
most of them returning home with nothing
but harsh memories and a speck of gold dust in a pill bottle—
none of those rowdy adventurers, those rainbow-enders,
thought it folly to chase such a dream.

Peace be to their ashes.

Richard S. Wheeler

After I'm Gone

Will she spread my ashes
down in the park, the Lamar Valley,
a place I loved where buffalo graze
beneath a cloud-patched sky
and wolves sun on distant ridges?

Or upon old precincts where history lives –
storied Virginia City, where I will mix with legend,
or Fort Benton on the high Missouri
where river boats brought men and disease
and shipped away innocence?

Will she scatter me upon the rocky banks
of the Yellowstone,
sweet wild river,
where the waters will tumble me
to the distant sea?

Or sprinkle a little of me among friends –
at Keith and Lucy's old farmhouse up Deep Creek,
in Tim and Linnea's back yard where dogs and stories romp,
at Alston and Diana's where we sipped eggnog
on a winter's eve?

Maybe at the Pine Creek Store where
I watched mountains, snows, and gold stubblefields –
or will she save the ash that was once me
and someday place it beside her own
at our home in the wide open West?

Paul Zarzyski

Cowboy Poet Barnstormer

> *Ain't no money in poetry*
> *That's what sets the poet free*
> *And I've had all the freedom*
> *I can stand.*
>
> —Guy Clark

Eighty-nine copies of your latest
alliterative lariati title
crammed, sans remaining space for one
anorectic, iambic molecule of mold or mildew,
in the Samsonite *Genuine Split Cowhide*
suitcase you wheedled
out of your widow neighbor in trade for
your soon-to-be-released CD
the night before her MOVING TO REST HOME
garage sale, you fly Loop-The-Loop Airlines
to your next big gig. In your head
you rehearse in Pig Latin
to make them interesting, the same ten
epic poems you remotely remember
writing eons ago. Their umpteen thousand
valium-melatonin cross
potency equivalent
clotheslines you into REM sleep
so primitive, you dream that you dream
the aft luggage hatch opens
forcefully as the prolapsed sphincter
of Pterodactyl rex. Your poetic fusillade
dumps and flutters down
like lutefisk and lefse on the land
of the other white meat outside Dubuque,

where dewlapped men in bibs
and rubber boots, after the storm, peel pages
off the sides of barns. Headlines
read: *PLUTONIUM SPACECRAFT BREAK-UP
OVER DUBUQUE SCATTERS DEBRIS*. You wake up
to the stewardesses *buh-bye, bub-eye,
buh-bye* refrain, sell two paperbacks
after your show, get wheedled into swapping,
copy for copy, four more
with slam cowboy poets from the Bronx, and swear
never, after a five a.m. black bean-
chorizo-goat cheese scramble,
to doze your way back east again.

—For Spike Barkin

Flowering

Their rump hairs puffed, chrysanthemum
antelope blossoms from beds
into morning hoarfrost, the rancid
scent of carnivore
boring through the frozen
air of their world
so perfectly sill.
                        His rifle propped,
rock-solid, crosshairs fixed
as if melded into the black-
haired face, why does the hunter stop
squeezing off the easy shot?
                              Not
because he's learned horned angels
germinate from earth
to save us from our own
cherubic ghosts—these animals
floating over rolling prairies of snow
like seraphim through cumulus.
                           Far less cosmic,
he stops because he feels his heart
refusing to march or charge
in uniform. At a pastoral stroll through rib
thicket, through flesh and Malone wool
and into a red-orange lichen coat
covering the boulder
he's layered against, warm waves thrum, then
pulsate back into him.
                         During this
nearly indiscernible blink
within his 45th winter, he yearns

for the fine tendrils of silence
crystalline air clings to,
most vitally, right before the rifle
fires.
      This instant, sunshine,
burning off the frost,
ignites the snapshot into action
time-lapse fast
toward a spring run-off
May morning in this very spot—antelope
browsing through wild iris and blue
lupine they all choose not to pick.

Photo Finish

Because a horse cannot see its own nose,
the bell mare stares at herself
mesmerized in the mirrored glass
vet clinic door—fixates so firmly
she's distracted from her chronic pain,
her herd-bound angst, her equine
gender's, shall we say, *testiness*? Deaf
to the duct tape's reptilian hiss
ripping off the roll—the vet
figure-eighting both front Styrofoam-padded hooves—
Cody, lulled by a million cc's curiosity,
balances passively on three legs
until, almost one wingbeat too soon, a finch,
flitting through her reflection, snaps
her out of her hipcocked hypnotic trance back to
her fractious self, pawing, snorting,
hell-bent to load up and haul home.
                                              Trailer
rocking a Richter-scale 6.8 on its hitch,
the Ford's floppy rearview tilts
just enough to force me to ponder,
glimpsing right, my own profile,
though, with one eye closed, *I can see*
pert-near around the prow of the nose
I've preferred all my life not
to regard too closely.
                            Pushing fifty now,
I take my cues from wise old Cody,
twice my age at twenty-five. I decide this,
indeed, is a Triple Crown nose, a nose
with run for the roses written all over it—thick

antithesis of *aquiline*, or even *equine*,
yet still reaching far enough beyond my hat brim
to absorb healthy photonic doses of solar vitamin D,
to make each and every oxygen molecule
feel especially welcomed. It's that kind
of in-with-the-good, out-with-the-bad
nose that discerns, blocks away,
fine cuisine from rancid grease,
alluring pheromones from cheap perfume,
music from boombox blare—our ears, admit it,
the worst of the five-senses-slackers
since the eyes accepted polyester.
                              Nostrils flared,
rhinoplasty be damned, this is *the* nose
for poetry, a prosodic nose, a nose that will
bulldog and bulldoze its way
to the flashbulbed finish line of life
where that unretouched snapshot will prove
arodynamically-challenged me
The Winner.

Reminders

Cocktail-hour autumn sun accents every cat-
scratched inch of short stroke, each
centimeter-deep groove
she racked into Ranch Oak
kitched table leg, a stick of asiago
cheese or frozen butter
a *Windows on the World* gourmet chef
shaved with fork tines
over a florid seafood dish
lightly garnished.
                  Blond wood shards on the dark
short-napped carpet, suddenly shagged
around this one table leg
the morning after, is what collared
our torrid nocturnal waltzer
curled in her cardboard box
near the wall heater and meowing
for her geriatric chow – the old
log house creaking as it warmed,
rousing from its own bad dreams of bear
claws honed cambium-deep
into living trees.
                Years after
our cat Georgia died, we peeled
wide vertical strips of tape
from the leg, refinished the rest
of the table, left this legacy as light-
hearted reminders of a simpler place
in time. Today, September 11, 2001,
I try to multiply that sadness of one
sudden absence of tiny life

by a cardinal number far too large,
far too unreal, for naming. Unable to render
my feeble grief into a single sliver of solace,
I am shaken, sipping a stiff drink,
by the image of all the living
victims' fingernails
shaken by the sight of all
bitten down to our painful quicks.

The Day Beelzebub Gave His Jezebel a Hotfoot

It was 53 below in Butte,
where they were marooned, after the hell-hole
it took them an eternity to drive up through
froze over, their fire-engine red Firebird
vapor-locking to a frigid halt
as they unwittingly drove beneath Our Lady
Of The Rockies – Snow White with an attitude,
all 90 feet and 80 steel tons of her
standing vigil over the Berkeley Pit.
        Red,
the mechanic at Red's Firebrand Texaco
tells the devil, *she ain't firin', no spark,*
Bub, and I'll be go-to-hell
if I can savvy what the hitch is
in your git-along-little-doggie,
not knowing, just how go-to-hell he'll truly be
if he doesn't get humorless Lucifer
back on the road, pronto. But how in hell
was Red supposed to know? The shrewd master
of disguise – tail, horns, cloven feet,
pointy ears and all – looked purt-near like most
like everyone else bundled up and ruddy-jowled
on just another colder than hell Butte
December afternoon.
      Hell-o, HELL-O!
Red heard ol' Diablo losing his cool
on the phone, deader than hell
for the seventh day straight. *Lord only knows*
when they'll get all the lines back up – ought to
change their handle from Ma Bell to Hell's Bells,
quips Red from underneath the hot rod

up to Satan, so much fire in his eyes
Red no longer needs his trouble light, nor does he
fully comprehend the severity of his faux-pas
as he rubs it in doubly deep with his
emphatic refrain, *Lord ONLY knows! Followed-up with:
this cold spell sure had been raisin' holy hell
around here this Christmas, and...JeeZUZ H. Key-RICE-st
on a crooked crutch...*Red didn't miss a beat,
oblivious to how timely was his exclamation,
Beelzebub's mood suddenly up-swung
with Red's good news of the netherworld's
crippled-up nemesis.

     *Hell-A-loolya
and here's to ya, my fumin' friend – I BY GOD
got your trouble pegged: your cataclysmic conundrum
mustta rubbed against your firewall, overheated,
and burnt your muffler valve
ALL TO HELL. Hope you're packin' a fire
extinguisher in this beast. Helluvanote, Bub,
but thank heaven I just happen to have the parts
to get you the hell-'n'-gone outta here.*   Beelzebub bit
hard on his barbed tongue to keep from saying
what a godsend! Then he forked over
the hot soft cash to pay Red's hellacious bill
while his fire-breathin' hellitosis grew
ranker than Red's restroom, fouler than the Prince
Albert tobacco tinful of hellgrammites
Red left on the dash after fishing
Wicked Crick. *Merry Christmas, Godspeed*, wishes Red
seemingly still oblivious to the blue smoke
plumes billowing from beneath
the hood Satan wore to hide his horns,
snowmelt pouring off the station's roof.

                              By now,
come hell or high water, Beelzebub is in
dire need of a Hades Boilermaker – a case of Heet
gasline deicer and a 3-fingers' (all he's got)
shot of Habanero Chile Pepper Schnapps. Back
at long last to the B & B (he thought it stood for
Beelzebub and Babe), he finds his beloved
bedazzling behemoth redhead buried
eyeball-(she's only got one) deep
beneath electric blankets turned all the way
to *HOT*. She's snoring her erotic snore
which brings ol' Beelzebub's blood to a brisk
molten lava boiling until he can't help but cave in
to his own temptations
until he catches a glimpse of her horny yellow
foot sticking through the stainless rails
and arousing him all to hell. The matchbook read
River Styx Hot Springs – Nether World, and Oh God!
Oh God! did Beelzebub's Jezebel ever have one
jump-start of an orgasmic jolt
that made the San Andreas Fault,
their second favorite vacation spot,
quaking 9.8 on the Richter Scale
seem like an infinitesimal jiggle, a flinch,
a dust mite's climax.
                       As they jubilantly sped
out of Butte, two helmeted apparitions
dressed horn-to-hoof in Halloween orange
and packing firearms for the late elk hunt
passed them on Hellcat snowmobiles
making Beelzebub lonesome for his own
florescent bed of coals. And you can bet

the magnetic glow-in-the-dark Saint Christopher
medal sly ol' Red slapped under the dash
that not even 666 eons of global warming,
complete with 666 hell ninos
plus two free passes to the Helsinki bathhouse
will ever tempt Beelzebub
to make his Jezebel, Helena, come here again.

> —For Ed Lahey, Rick and Carole DeMarinis,
> and Ed McClanahan

Time Travel

Gravel roads into a black hole
canopy of hardwood forest
were all the secrets of the cosmos
she and I craved in those days
before compact cars. We made aerobic love
in the king-size back seat of a '56 Buick
Roadmaster—pink Buck Rogers rocket ship
I flew with one finger locked cool
to the fuchsia suicide knob while she clung so close
we exchanged our hearts' accelerated drum
solos like the last all-out heat
in a battle-of-the-bands. Flying fast as
teenage foreplay to our parking spot, our high
beams nipping recklessly at the heels of risk,
we turned our eyes from the road
for a breathless kiss, miles long. It's been eons
since I've glimpsed the red needle's defiance
to the right, and now, climbing past 95,
rushing home the emergency serum
for the fevered mare that so easily foaled
but cannot slip her afterbirth—now,
with old thrills relived for this instant,
should I regret my childless life,
the way we dreaded pregnancy
back then? How ironically we chanced sparking
new life in our quest to test death. Yet,
what if speed now was for my own flesh
and blood anxious within a young wife? Or what if
this two-lane pavement turned
suddenly to gravel and dust rooster tails
churning in the rear-view,

this rolling prairie to elm and oak,
and this daylight to just one more dark
night's play of rhythm-method
roulette around the old back road to Omar's
Park with her? Slowing down to 110,
I think *What love. What luck.* But
coming to a whiplash stop,
to the engine's frenzied ticking, I wonder
is it ever luck at all, and if
it is, then how long, I ask,
does luck's half-life last?

Contributors

Mike Blakely is the author of fifteen historical novels set in the American West and the winner of the coveted Spur Award for fiction. A songwriter and performer, Blakely tours with his band internationally and hosts his own literary and music festival every September in Luckenbach, Texas. He raises paint horses and lives on a ranch in Texas.

Laurie Wagner Buyer, poet, novelist, and memoirist, received an MFA in Writing from Goddard College. When she is not backpacking in the high country or on the road performing, speaking, and presenting workshops, she lives in Woodland Park, Colorado, where she devotes time to mentoring other writers.

Jon Chandler is a novelist, songwriter, and poet. With several CDs to his credit, he performs regularly throughout the American West and is the winner of the Best First Novel Award presented by the Western Writers of America. Chandler lives in Westminster, Colorado.

Bob Cherry is an award-winning poet and novelist and his short fiction has appeared in numerous publications. His fourth novel, *Little Rains*, was selected by the *Denver Post* as one of the ten most notable books of 2003. Cherry writes from his ranch sixty miles east of Yellowstone.

Gaydell Collier is the co-editor of three anthologies, three books on horses and horsemanship, and her work has been published in numerous periodicals and anthologies. Collier lives on a horse ranch in Wyoming's Black Hills where she pursues her interests in writing, ranching, horses, dogs, the land, grand opera, and dark chocolate.

John Duncklee has served in the Navy, been a cowhand, a rancher, a college professor, and a designer and builder of custom mesquite furniture. He has been a free lance writer for thirty-five years and has authored ten books since 1994. He lives in Las Cruces, New Mexico.

Dan Guenther is the author of a novel, *China Wind*, based on his combat tour in Vietnam, and *High Country Solitudes*, a volume of poetry based on his experiences in the American West. Guenther was a captain in the U.S. Marine Corps, and has a Masters of Fine Arts in English from the University of Iowa.

Linda Hussa, writer and rancher in the Great Basin, has three poetry collections and three books of nonfiction. The themes of her work are drawn from the isolated nature of ranching, the commitment to the rural community, and to the creatures of the land. Her collection of poetry, *Blood Sister, I Am To These Fields*, won the Spur Award from the Western Writers of America, the Wrangler Award from the Western Heritage Museum, and the WILLA from Women Writing the West.

W.C. Jameson is an award-winning author of over fifty books and 1500 published essays and articles. In addition to writing, he has earned his living variously as a musician, disc jockey, kickboxer, artist, rodeo performer, dockworker, actor, and college professor. He divides his time between the deserts and hill country of Texas and the Colorado Rockies.

Celinda Kaelin is a poet, author, lecturer, and historian. She works and studies with indigenous Elders and spiritual leaders from over forty nations, has performed earth-healing ceremonies in North and South America, and is a member of the World Council of Elders. Her Lakota name is *Sunkmanitou Wi* and she lives with her husband on a ranch in Florissant, Colorado.

Page Lambert received a 2004 Literary Fellowship in Poetry from the Wyoming Arts Council, has authored a memoir and novel, and her essays have appeared in numerous anthologies. Lambert divides her time between Denver, Colorado, and Santa Fe, New Mexico.

Max McCoy is a novelist, investigative journalist, and screenwriter. He has authored twelve books, including four original Indiana Jones novels for Lucasfilm. He is a winner of the Medicine Pipe Bearer Award for Best First Novel, the Oxbow Award for short fiction, and a three-time winner for investigative reporting from the Missouri Press Association and the Associated Press.

Red Shuttleworth's poems have been published in a number of important journals. His book *Western Settings* received the 2001 Spur Award for Best Western Poetry. His latest play, *When It Goes Haywire*, was produced by the Foothill Theater Company in California with support from the National Endowment for the Arts.

George Sibley teaches journalism and organizes conferences at Western State College in Gunnison, Colorado. His essays and articles have appeared in *Harper's Magazine, High Country News, Mountain Gazette, True West,* and *Colorado Central,* and he has authored one book. He lives in the Upper Gunnison river valley.

Larry D. Thomas was born and raised in West Texas and writes in Houston and Galveston. He has published four collections of poems. *Amazing Grace* won a 2003 Western Heritage Award, the Texas Review Poetry Prize, and was a finalist for the Spur Award for Best Western Poetry.

Mark Todd teaches creative writing at Western State College in Gunnison, Colorado. His first collection of poetry, *Wire Song*, was published in 2001. His poems have appeared in numerous publications and anthologies, and he is working on a second collection featuring narrative and lyrical poetry about the New and Old West.

He lives with his wife near Gunnison, where they raise and train horses.

Lori Van Pelt is an award-winning writer whose works have appeared in regional and national publications. Her collection of short fiction, *At Frontier's Edge: A Biographical History*, was published by the University of New Mexico Press, and her biography of Amelia Earhart was published by Forge Books. Lori lives with her husband on his family's ranch near Saratoga, Wyoming.

Dale L. Walker has authored numerous books on Western and military history, is a four-time winner of the Spur Award, and in 2000 received the Owen Wister Award for lifetime contribution to Western history and literature. Dale lives in El Paso, Texas.

Richard S. Wheeler is a former newsman and book editor and has been a full-time novelist for two decades. He writes novels of the American West. Wheeler is a four-time winner of the Spur Award presented for best western fiction, and is the recipient of the Owen Wister Award for his contributions to the literature of the American West. He lives in Livingston, Montana.

Paul Zarzyski is a veteran of fifteen seasons as a bareback rider on the rodeo circuit, the author of eight books, and the winner of the prestigious Western Heritage Award and Spur Award for his poetry. He has also recorded two spoken-word discs. He performs throughout the United States as well as in Great Britain and Australia and lives near Great Falls, Montana.

Printed in the United States
76375LV00005B/253-381